TOP 10 HAUNTED PUBS UK

Welcome to our countdown of the top 10 most haunted pubs in Britain.
Together, we'll explore British pubs and taverns famous for their ghostly histories and mysterious happenings.
Here are the pubs that bring Britain's spookiest ghost stories to life.

Number 10:
The Ostrich Inn, Colnbrook,

It is often claimed to be the third oldest pub in England, but this claim has never been substantiated.

The Ostrich Inn in Colnbrook, near Slough, dates to 1106, the reign of Henry I. At that time, it was called "The Hospice."

Visitors today can still witness and marvel at some of the pub's medieval features, which add to its historic charm.

Legend has it that King John stayed at this inn in 1215 on his way to Runnymede to seal the Magna Carta.

Eventually, its name changed to "The Ostrich," though few people had likely ever seen the exotic bird in medieval England.

Some believe the original name might have been "The Oyster Ridge" or "The Eastridge," which could have morphed into "The Ostrich" over time. I like that 'Ostrich' and 'Hospice' would sound remarkably the same after a skinful of ale.

Let's journey back to that very inn in the 17th century and learn of a chilling tale of betrayal and murder, said to inspire the story of Sweeney Todd, the demon barber of Fleet Street.

The Ostrich Inn was a high-quality establishment, drawing a wealthier class of guests who sought comfortable lodgings along the main route between London and Bath.

This steady influx of affluent travellers made the inn a prime target for criminals of all sorts—highway robbers, footpads, and pickpockets—who saw the opportunity to prey upon guests with valuable belongings.

Highwaymen, notorious for their ambushes along England's rural roads, often lurked near inns like The Ostrich, waiting for wealthy patrons to leave in the early morning or late evening.

Footpads, known for mugging pedestrians, also haunted the paths around Colnbrook, hoping to catch travellers off guard under the cover of darkness.

Inside the inn, pickpockets and confidence tricksters mingled with the guests, posing as fellow travellers or locals to initiate friendly conversations. They would subtly observe their marks, noting who carried coin purses or other valuables and plan their schemes accordingly.

Some even used charm and deception, cosying up to their targets over a drink only to steal from them when distracted.

One tale tied to The Ostrich Inn is that of the infamous highwayman Dick Turpin, who allegedly hid here to escape the authorities. It is said that a keeper of a toll house was fatally shot.

Witnesses reported seeing Turpin in The Ostrich. He was known as a notorious burglar, horse thief, and murderer, but he escaped capture by leaping from one of the inn's windows to be famously caught some time later and hanged for horse theft.

The constant risk of such attacks led many patrons to exercise caution, carry concealed weapons, or hire guards for added protection.

John Jarman and his wife were among the rogues who preyed on guests of The Ostrich, but the couple had the best advantage over everyone:

They owned the establishment and were the landlord and landlady.

They weren't your average convivial hosts; they were an evil couple who devised a sinister scheme to supplement their income beyond serving ale, board, and lodgings.

The couple had a trapdoor built into one of the inn's bedrooms, intending to use it for their wealthy guests.

Sometimes, spotting a well-to-do target was easy once they'd brushed off the dust and grime of travelling.

Imagine, in the dim glow of the inn's flickering candles, a man sits alone at a sturdy oak table, his posture upright and presence subtly commanding.

He is well-dressed, each piece of his attire hinting at a prosperous and dynamic life.

His fine, dark velvet doublet with discreet silver embroidery along the seams speaks of wealth without ostentation.
The fitted jacket rests over a crisp linen shirt, its ruffled cuffs peeking below his sleeves. It is meticulously pressed and spotless, marking him as a man of some refinement.

A wide-brimmed hat sits on the table beside his half-finished tankard of ale. Its brim is feathered with a single plume, adding a flourish of style that hints at a touch of vanity.

This fine gentleman would be their perfect target, wealthy and alone. Generally, such travellers carried a bundle of essential and valuable documents, including their will, promissory notes, deeds, etc.

A skinful of ale, a good deal of fine wine and perhaps several glugs of spirits courtesy of the monks, plus a sprinkle of some dodgy sleeping compound made by the local Apothecary (no questions asked), would knock out the victim and allow quick and easy access to anything or everything that had a value.

John Jarman and his wife's code was simple yet darkly effective: when a suitably prosperous guest arrived,

Jarman would say, "My dearest, there is now a fat pig to be had if you desire." She replied, "I pray you put him in the hogsty till the morrow."
Unaware of the grim fate awaiting them, the guest would fall asleep comfortably, with help from the Jarmans, after being directed to a "special room."

Under the bed was a trapdoor leading to a cauldron of boiling water or fat below. Once the guest was asleep, Jarman pulled a lever, and they would drop through the trapdoor, ending his life in the boiling pot.

The couple would then sell the victim's belongings to local gypsies and dispose of the remains in a nearby brook.

Their grisly scheme unravelled when they targeted Thomas Cole, a well-known cloth merchant. They even persuaded him to rewrite his will under the influence, or they altered the will themselves.

After his murder, Cole's horse had somehow escaped, probably due to interference and theft of the bridle and saddle.

It had roamed the streets, leading locals to believe Cole had fallen.

A search was launched, and suspicion fell on the inn. When Cole's altered will was discovered, Jarman fled but was eventually captured, hiding in Windsor Forest. Both he and his wife confessed to 60 murders. They were tried and sentenced to be hanged.

Cole's body was later recovered from the brook behind the Ostrich Inn, and folklore suggests that Colnbrook was named after this event—originally "Cole-in-the-Brook."

The Ostrich Inn is rumoured to be haunted, and its hauntings are well-documented. Guests and staff alike have reported unsettling experiences at the inn, from glimpses of ghostly figures to objects mysteriously shifting on their own.

Cold spots are frequently felt in the ladies' restroom—rumoured to have been where Jarman hid bodies—as well as in the dining area adjacent to the notorious "murder room."

Visitors often describe an overwhelming sense of dread upon entering that room. Sightings of a woman dressed in Victorian attire and a young girl add to the inn's eerie atmosphere, their spectral presence lingering and enhancing the haunting ambience of the historic inn.

Number 9:
The Viaduct Tavern

The Viaduct Tavern: The City of London's Most Haunted Pub.

Nestled across from the Old Bailey, officially known as the Central Criminal Court, the Viaduct Tavern has earned a notorious reputation as one of London's most haunted pubs.

With a history steeped in lore and lingering spirits, this Victorian-era establishment has witnessed enough paranormal activity to secure its place among London's most chilling sites.

Constructed between 1872 and 1875, the Viaduct Tavern was named after the nearby Holborn Viaduct, built as part of the grand Holborn Valley Improvement scheme.

This project replaced some of London's most infamous slums, including Field Lane and Saffron Hill Rookery, which were notorious for their crime. Charles Dickens immortalized it in Oliver Twist as the setting of Fagin's lair.

Despite popular myth, the pub's cellars are not the remains of the infamous Newgate Prison, which once stood across the road from where the Old Bailey now resides.

Although many love the idea of the basement being a holding cell for criminals, no prisoners were ever kept there.

However, the proximity to Newgate, where public executions were held until 1868, seems to have cast a long shadow, with echoes of its grim history—and perhaps spirits of the condemned—still lingering in and around the tavern.

Over the years, the site has hosted various businesses, from an 1823 printer's shop accused of "blasphemous libel" to the London Friendly Institution of Mechanics in the 1830s.

Even remnants of ancient Roman walls were unearthed here during construction, adding an extra layer of history and mystery to the pub's foundations.

Today, much of the Viaduct Tavern's 19th-century decor remains intact. Ornate plaster ceilings, gleaming cut-glass accents, and classical figures depicted in murals are testaments to the Victorian era's competitive quest for grand pub interiors.

One of these features even holds its dark legend: the central panel in a mural is said to have been slashed by a soldier's bayonet during World War I.

The tales of the Viaduct Tavern's haunting
began in the 1970s when regulars started
sharing stories of strange occurrences.
One of the most famous hauntings
happened in 1981 when the landlord's
daughter, alone in the pub during a
mandatory afternoon closure, heard heavy
footsteps on the stairs.

Suddenly, the door flew open, a newspaper was snatched from her hands, and the door slammed shut, yet no trace of anyone was ever found.

Soon, the tavern's resident ghost earned the nickname "Fred." Throughout the 1980s and 90s, Fred's pranks became part of the pub's lore.

He would drain patrons' drinks when they weren't looking, flick lights on and off, and flush the ladies' room toilet at inconvenient times.

Patrons and staff grew accustomed to his antics, often offering a free drink to those startled by Fred's mischief.

The pub's cellar, however, holds a particularly eerie reputation. In 1996, a manager was tidying up when the cellar door suddenly slammed shut and the lights went out.

No matter how hard he tried, he couldn't open the door. Fortunately, his wife heard his shouts and found the door unlocked and easy to open from the outside.

The incident only intensified the tavern's haunted reputation.

In 1997, a local news station featured the Viaduct Tavern for a Halloween special, bringing a medium to assess the hauntings.

Upon arrival, the medium informed the staff that the ghost's actual name was Robert—not Fred—and he was "not amused" by the nickname.

Reports of strange activity continued into the late 1990s, including an incident involving two electricians who felt taps on their shoulders and witnessed a heavy carpet mysteriously lift and drop on its own.

To this day, Fred—or Robert—remains an active presence.

Sudden temperature drops, unexplained noises from the cellar, and the unpredictable activation of hand dryers in the bathrooms are all part of the Viaduct Tavern's ghostly charm.

Humorous bathroom signs warn patrons of these occurrences, courtesy of the tavern's mischievous spectral resident.

With its rich history, original decor, and reputation for haunted hospitality, the Viaduct Tavern is a must-visit for those intrigued by the paranormal.

Whether you come for the ambience, the history, or a chance encounter with Fred, this pub offers an unforgettable glimpse into London's haunted past.

Number 8:
Ye Olde Man and Scythe

Ye Olde Man & Scythe is one of Bolton's most famous landmarks and among the oldest pubs in the UK.

This historic inn, standing in Churchgate since the 12th century, has witnessed centuries of history and, according to legend, is haunted by numerous spirits, including that of James Stanley, the 7th Earl of Derby.

The first recorded mention of the pub dates to 1251, when a Royal Charter was issued, allowing a market to be held on the property, which the Earl of Derby owned at the time.

Over the years, the pub has seen various renovations, showing a date stone indicating that it was rebuilt in 1636.

However, portions of the cellar are believed to date to the original medieval structure.

The pub's name and signage—a man holding a scythe—have a storied origin.

Around the time of the Royal Charter in 1251, property ownership passed from the Ferrers family, Earls of Derby, to the Pilkington through marriage.

The Pilkington family crest, depicting a man with a scythe, is said to honour a family legend from the Norman Conquest era, when an ancestor allegedly disguised himself as a farmer to evade capture.

Over time, this symbolic scythe became synonymous with the pub itself.

The Pilkingtons' loyalty to the English crown during the Wars of the Roses led to further connections with the site. Sir Thomas Pilkington, a Yorkist supporter of Richard III, fought at the Battle of Bosworth in 1485, where the Yorkist forces were defeated.

After the battle, Henry VII granted the Pilkington estate to Thomas Stanley, a vital supporter of the Tudor claim.

Thus, the earldom returned to the Stanley family, marking a significant turn in the pub's history.

Ye Olde Man & Scythe became central to one of the bloodiest chapters in Bolton's history during the English Civil War. On May 28, 1644, Royalist forces, led by Prince Rupert of the Rhine and supported by James Stanley, 7th Earl of Derby, stormed Bolton, resulting in the massacre of approximately 1,500 people, including soldiers and civilians.

Much of the bloodshed unfolded in the streets surrounding the pub, embedding it with a dark and violent legacy.

The Earl's connection to Ye Olde Man & Scythe would grow even more profound. After the war, Stanley was arrested, tried for treason, and sentenced to execution for his role in the massacre.

The Earl's connection to Ye Olde Man & Scythe would grow even more profound.

After the war, Stanley was arrested, tried for treason, and sentenced to execution for his role in the massacre.

On October 15, 1651, he was brought to Bolton, where he had a final meal with the landlord, James Cockrel, before his execution. Stanley was beheaded outside the pub at 3:00 p.m., making Ye Olde Man & Scythe the final setting of his life.

The chair he sat in before his execution, a Flemish piece dating back to 1590, still resides in the pub's Museum Room, where visitors can see this relic from the past.

According to lore, the chair was damaged in 1965, although it remains unclear whether an evil ghost caused it.

Ye Olde Man & Scythe has a reputation as one of Britain's most haunted pubs. Tales of at least 20 restless spirits said to inhabit its walls.

Among them is the ghost of James Stanley, 7th Earl of Derby, whose apparition has been seen in the Museum Room.

He appears seated in silent contemplation, perhaps reliving his last moments before his tragic execution.

His presence seems to be a sad reminder of the pub's violent history and the events leading up to his death.

Another notable spirit believed to haunt the pub is Jenny, a young girl who reportedly roams the passageways.

Guests and staff alike have felt her presence; some catch glimpses of her shadow darting through the halls, while others report a sudden tug on their clothing or even a playful pinch.

The spirit of a small boy is also seen sporadically throughout the building, though his identity remains a mystery, adding an eerie element to his appearance.

Beyond these figures, paranormal encounters at Ye Olde Man & Scythe include objects moving independently, sudden, inexplicable chills, and the unmistakable sensation of being watched.

Disembodied voices echo through the rooms, and visitors frequently report shadowy figures passing by, only to disappear when approached.

One particularly chilling account comes from a visitor who, during her stay, felt her hands grow icy and tingle, only to glance down and see them covered in blood—a vision that vanished within moments, leaving her shaken. With its rich history, supernatural legends, and spine-tingling occurrences, Ye Olde Man & Scythe draws paranormal enthusiasts, curious travellers, and history lovers alike.

The pub stands not only as a reminder of England's tumultuous past but also as a place where the echoes of history seem to linger long after the living have departed. For those brave enough to visit, it offers a rare and unforgettable chance to interact with spirits of bygone eras, making it a must-see for anyone seeking a truly haunted experience in the heart of Bolton.

Number 7:
The Mermaid Inn

The Mermaid Inn in East Sussex boasts a rich history dating back to the 12th century.

The main structure was rebuilt in 1420, with further additions in the 16th century.

While only the cellars of the original building remain, the inn is deeply connected to the notorious Hawkhurst Smuggler Gang, whose infamous presence is believed to be linked to many of the hauntings that give the inn its spectral reputation.

The inn's haunted history is most evident in specific rooms where ghostly activity has been repeatedly witnessed.

Grey ladies or ladies in white are famous sightings in many haunted buildings, and The Mermaid is no exception.

 In Room 1, also known as The James, visitors have reported seeing a lady dressed in white or grey, seated quietly by the fireplace, her gaze fixed as if lost in memories.

Room 16 is reputed to have been the site of a deadly duel, and some guests claim that the spirits involved continue to re-enact the clash, with the room's atmosphere turning tense and unnervingly cold.

Room 17 is home to the spirit of a 16th-century smuggler's wife, whose ghostly presence harks back to when Rye was still a thriving port.

In addition to these rooms, other ghostly figures have been seen wandering the inn's historic halls.

Another "white lady" has been observed crossing a room, only to stop at the foot of a bed, seemingly watching over whoever lies there.

Guests have also reported an apparition of a man who appears in the bathroom, walks calmly through its wall, and disappears into the main room.

The paranormal activity isn't limited to apparitions. In the Elizabethan Chamber, guests and staff have witnessed bottles inexplicably crashing to the floor, often without apparent cause.

The sensation of being watched, sudden cold spots, and mysterious sounds are frequent, adding to the inn's eerie charm.

The Mermaid Inn is a relic of England's storied past, where centuries of history, smuggling, and spectral legends converge.

For those who venture here, the inn offers more than just a night's stay; it provides an immersive experience in a place where history and the supernatural blend, creating an unforgettable—and often chilling—experience.

Whether drawn by its history or hauntings, visitors to The Mermaid Inn will surely leave with their tales.

Number 6:
The Jamaica Inn

Returning to the 18th century, Jamaica Inn was a vital stop for weary travellers journeying the turnpike road between Bodmin and Launceston.

Its name comes from the influential Trelawney family, prominent landowners in the area.

Two of them served as Governors of Jamaica during that era.

Nestled within the rugged expanse of Bodmin Moor, the inn provided essential shelter and sustenance for those braving the wind-battered landscape.

However, its walls also harboured a darker side, as it became a favoured haunt for smugglers and outlaws who sought refuge in the isolated reaches of Cornwall.

The Jamaica Inn achieved international fame in 1936 with the release of Daphne du Maurier's novel 'Jamaica Inn,' a tale of smuggling and intrigue set against Cornwall's wild backdrop.

Du Maurier's portrayal of the inn as a place of mystery and danger captured readers' imaginations, attracting visitors from across the globe and transforming the historic inn into the atmospheric establishment that continues to captivate guests today.

Many believe spirits still roam the Jamaica Inn's dimly lit corridors and shadowy rooms.

Visitors often report the sound of phantom footsteps echoing down the hallways late at night, as if someone from centuries past is making their rounds.

Outside, the ghostly clatter of horses' hooves is sometimes heard in the courtyard during the early morning hours.

Curious yet cautious, guests peek through their curtains to find an eerie silence and an empty yard.

Some guests have claimed to hear murmurs of intense conversations in a strange, almost forgotten dialect—perhaps a reminder of the inn's smuggling heritage.

Yet the most famous spirit linked to Jamaica Inn is the ghost of a lone wanderer.

As the story goes, this traveller was quietly enjoying his ale at the bar many years ago when a dark figure appeared in the doorway, beckoning him outside.

Setting down his half-full tankard, the man ventured into the night, never to return. His body was discovered on the moor the following day, leaving his identity and the story of his death shrouded in mystery.

Since then, his spectral form has been seen countless times near the inn's front wall, sitting in silence, lost in thought. He remains oblivious to passersby, and after a few moments of gazing distantly, he gradually fades into nothingness.

For those who visit today, the Jamaica Inn offers more than a stay—it promises an experience steeped in history, mystery, and perhaps a brush with the supernatural.

Whether drawn by the intrigue of its ghostly legends or the allure of Cornwall's untamed beauty, visitors to Jamaica Inn find themselves stepping back in time, surrounded by the whispers of its smuggling past and the lingering spirits of those who once walked its halls.

Number 5:
The Red Lion, Avebury.

The Red Lion Inn is unique, alone as the only pub within a prehistoric stone circle. The ancient stones of Avebury, dating from between 4000 and 2400 BC, form three concentric circles around the inn, adding an aura of mystique to the Red Lion's thatched, whitewashed walls.

Originally built as a farmhouse in the early 1600s, the building was converted into a coaching inn in 1802, providing respite to travellers navigating the rugged countryside roads.

Today, the inn caters to weary travellers and those drawn to Avebury's legendary blend of magic and mystery.

According to legend, this ominous sight is a harbinger of tragedy, foretelling the death of a close relative of anyone who witnesses it.

Understandably, past landlords have yet to be eager to see this phantom visitor. Inside, the inn's most well-known ghost is Florrie, whose tragic tale dates back to the 17th-century English Civil War.

As the story goes, Florrie's husband returns home unexpectedly from the battlefield.

He finds her in the arms of another man.

In a fit of rage, he killed her lover and then slit Florrie's throat. Dragging her body to the inn's well—still visible within the pub—he threw her down and sealed it with a massive boulder.

Florrie's spirit, they say, remains at the Red Lion, forever seeking a bearded man.

Some say she's searching for her husband; others believe she seeks her lost lover. Guests have reportedly seen her emerge from and disappear into the well, now serving as a glass-covered drinks table for curious patrons.

Florrie seems to have a particular interest in bearded visitors, often singling them out.

One famous story recounts when a man with a bushy beard was seated beneath a chandelier in the dining area.

The pub's manager, noticing the guest's beard, gave a knowing nod—another indication of Florrie's lingering presence.

Other spirits also haunt the Red Lion's ancient rooms, most notably in the Avenue Bedroom. Here, guests have reported seeing two ghostly children huddled together in a corner as though frightened.

A woman, possibly a mother figure, is often seen nearby, absorbed in writing at a table, seemingly indifferent to the children's distress.

Their identities and the tragedy that binds them to this place remain shrouded in mystery, secrets held tight by the inn's silent, sturdy walls.

Beyond these spectral figures, visitors frequently encounter other strange phenomena: orbs of light hovering in darkened corners,

shadows dancing across walls, and sudden cold spots that leave even the most sceptical guests unsettled.

Some have found their experiences so unnerving that they refuse to stay another night.

Despite the tales of ghostly encounters, the Red Lion remains a beloved destination, enchanting guests with its blend of history, mystery, and timeless charm.

For those who believe—or hope to believe—the Red Lion offers a truly extraordinary experience amidst the ancient stones of Avebury.

Number 4:
The Skirrid Inn, Wales.

Nestled beneath the shadow of Skirrid Mountain, The Skirrid Mountain Inn in Wales holds a chilling and storied past. Initially, the inn's upper floor served as a courtroom where those accused of severe crimes faced swift judgment and, in many cases, were sentenced to death.

According to legend, over 180 felons met their end here, walking from the courtroom through a nearby doorway to be hanged from a thick rope slung over a sturdy oak beam above the staircase.

Today, markings from the hangman's rope remain etched into the wood—a grim reminder of lives lost within the inn's walls.

One of the inn's most notorious figures is the 17th-century "Hanging Judge," George Jeffreys, whose reputation for harsh sentences earned him a fearsome legacy.

His spirit is said to linger on the upper floors, restlessly wandering the halls and searching for new souls to condemn.

Many guests report feeling unsettling, as though they're being watched or judged, as Jeffreys' ghost casts a cold shadow over the building. Historical records show that 182 individuals were hanged from the same beam, and it's believed that many of these souls remain trapped within the inn, reliving their final, fateful moments.

Another infamous spirit associated with the inn is that of John Crowther, a sheep rustler sentenced to death at Skirrid.

His apparition has been spotted multiple times near the staircase, where he took his final steps. A darker presence, thought to be the hangman himself, has also been encountered, adding to the inn's sinister reputation and heightening its ghostly legends.

Not all spirits at the Skirrid Inn are evil, however.

Father Henry Vaughn, a kind-hearted clergyman, is said to linger within, bringing a gentle and calming energy to the otherwise haunted atmosphere.

Another familiar presence is Fanny Price, a young woman who worked at the inn in the 18th century and died of consumption at age 35.

Her spirit is particularly drawn to Room 3, often heralded by the delicate scent of lavender, her favourite fragrance, which drifts through the air as she makes her presence known.

The inn has seen its share of terrifying encounters. In one alarming incident, a female guest came running downstairs, soaked and wrapped in a coat, shouting, "She tried to kill me!" She claimed that an unseen force had held her under the water while she was bathing.

Similar eerie episodes have been reported throughout the years, with inexplicable cold spots, sudden intense fear, and overwhelming sensations of panic among the everyday experiences of visitors and staff.

One former landlady, attempting to sell the inn, encountered relentless poltergeist activity that seemed to resist her every effort to transfer ownership.

During one property viewing, glasses in the kitchen reportedly shattered and flew across the room as if protesting the presence of potential buyers.

Other supernatural disturbances include the sound of a woman's dress rustling through the inn. In the courtyard, some guests have heard the faint sounds of soldiers, reminders of the inn's ties to wartime history, while the elusive "White Lady" has often been glimpsed, her quiet, ghostly form drifting through the rooms.

The Skirrid Mountain Inn is a historic landmark and magnet for paranormal enthusiasts today.

Visitors come hoping to connect with its haunted past, and many leave with unforgettable stories of their own, forever touched by the spirits that linger within its walls.

For those who dare to spend a night, the Skirrid Inn offers a rare and thrilling experience—a step back to witness echoes of its dark, centuries-old history.

Number 3:
The Golden Fleece

The Golden Fleece Inn is one of the most historic pubs in York and has a reputation for being one of the most haunted buildings in the UK.

This centuries-old inn dates back to at least the early 16th century. It has witnessed a long and fascinating history and has become a destination for locals, tourists, and even paranormal enthusiasts.

While its rich history alone is captivating, the Golden Fleece is perhaps best known for its extensive roster of ghostly residents—at least 15 spirits are said to call the inn home, adding a spooky allure that few other establishments can rival.

Visitors to the Golden Fleece have reported various paranormal experiences.

From witnessing apparitions to feeling cold drafts, hearing mysterious voices, and even experiencing the touch of invisible hands.

Such experiences have attracted the attention of paranormal investigators and curious tourists alike.

The Golden Fleece was originally a coaching inn located in York's historic heart. Its earliest record dates to 1503, and it has functioned as a beloved pub and inn ever since.

During the English Civil War, it reportedly served as a meeting place for Royalists.

The inn's history also includes visits from infamous figures like the highwayman Dick Turpin.

Over the years, murders and suicides have further contributed to the inn's haunted lore, and renovations as recent as 2000 have uncovered relics like a 200-year-old bathroom, adding more layers to its already fascinating history.

Among the Golden Fleece's most famous spirits is One-Eyed Jack, a ghost believed to be a former innkeeper or smuggler.

Jack appears in a red 16th-century coat and carries a pistol.

Multiple guests and staff members have seen him in areas such as the bottom bar and cellar, and his single-eyed gaze and old-fashioned attire leave an indelible impression on those who encounter him.

Another well-known spirit is Lady Alice Peckett, the wife of a former mayor of York.

Lady Peckett is frequently spotted wandering the halls in an elegant 18th-century dress, seemingly searching for something lost in time.

Some guests report feeling her presence in their rooms or catching glimpses of her reflection in mirrors.

Her dignified figure is often described as both regal and mournful, enhancing the inn's haunted atmosphere.

In addition to these famous apparitions, the Golden Fleece hosts a range of lesser-known spirits.

Among them is a Canadian airman who died during World War II. His ghost is sometimes seen in full uniform on the upper floors.

Another spectral resident is a ghostly cat that roams the halls, meowing softly before vanishing into thin air.

The ghost of a young girl, believed to be the daughter of a former landlord, has also been seen in the cellar, often accompanied by playful giggles.

With centuries-old architecture, connections to York's colourful past, and an array of ghost stories that will send chills down your spine, this inn is a unique destination for those drawn to the supernatural.

Number 2:
The Spaniards Inn

The Spaniards Inn, situated on Spaniards Road in Hampstead, London, is a historic pub with roots tracing back to the 16th century.

Built around 1585, it originally served as a tollgate inn on the border of the Bishop of London's estate.

Over the centuries, the inn has gained a reputation not only as a quaint landmark but also as a refuge for infamous characters, most notably the notorious highwayman Dick Turpin, (yes, him again!) who is said to have used the inn as a hideout in the 18th century.

The Spaniards Inn is also renowned for its paranormal history, rich with ghostly encounters reported by patrons and staff alike.

One of the most frequently sighted spirits is that of a former landlord known as Black Dick. Witnesses often describe him as a shadowy figure who appears unexpectedly, creating a chill in the air.

Some patrons claim to have felt his presence brush past them or experience sudden cold spots throughout the building, as though he is silently watching the premises.

Another spirit rumoured to haunt the inn is that of Bella, a Spanish barmaid. According to legend, a jealous admirer tragically murdered Bella, and her spirit now lingers in the pub, perhaps searching for closure.

Visitors frequently report hearing unexplained footsteps when the rooms are empty or catching fleeting glimpses of a woman in period dress.

Bella's presence is said to carry an air of melancholy, adding to the inn's haunting atmosphere.

The ghost of Dick Turpin himself is also rumoured to wander the vicinity.

On certain nights, guests have claimed to see his spectral figure on horseback nearby or hear the unmistakable sound of galloping hooves echoing down the quiet road as though Turpin is still fleeing from his pursuers.

In the inn's garden, visitors occasionally encounter the ghost of a woman in white, thought to be connected to a centuries-old duel that allegedly took place there.

Her pale figure is sometimes spotted near the garden's edge, and guests have reported hearing the faint sound of clashing swords and distant cries as if the tragic confrontation is replaying in time.

Throughout the pub's long history, staff and patrons have experienced a range of unexplained phenomena.

The Spaniards Inn is a historic landmark and a living monument to the spirits that linger within its walls.

For those who visit, the pub offers an experience steeped in legend, mystery, and a touch of the supernatural—a reminder that the past, with all its drama and intrigue, may never truly be gone.

Number 1:
The Grenadier Inn, London

Tucked away in the charming, cobbled enclave of Wilton Mews, far from the bustle of modern London, lies one of the city's most atmospheric pubs:.

The Grenadier. Dating back to around 1720, the Grenadier began as an officers' mess for a nearby barracks and later became a drinking and gambling den for soldiers. It remains rich in history, haunted tales, and spectral mysteries.

The Grenadier's most enduring ghost story centres on a Junior Officer who was reportedly caught cheating at cards.

Legend has it that his comrades punished him so severely that he died from his injuries.

There is no record as to the exact year when this junior officer was killed, but it is believed he met his fate during a September—fittingly, the month when paranormal activity at the pub seems to peak.

During this time, visitors and staff frequently report an increase in ghostly encounters.

These include: the appearance of a solemn, shadowy figure gliding across the low-ceilinged rooms to the sudden chill that lingers in certain areas.

The sound of footsteps pacing the empty rooms is often heard, along with faint, mournful sighs rising from the depths of the cellar.

On one memorable occasion, a Chief Superintendent from New Scotland Yard was enjoying a quiet drink.

Suddenly wisps of smoke began to swirl around him.

Reaching out, he felt a sharp burn like he had touched an invisible cigarette.

Former head barman Greyam Fox, who worked at the Grenadier from 1982 to 1983, recalls his unsettling encounters with the pub's resident ghost, whom he affectionately dubbed "Cedric."

One winter's night, while fetching cigars from the cellar, he felt an abrupt drop in temperature.

Suddenly, the pub's friendly black cat, Bobby, whom he thought was confined to the landlord's flat, appeared out of nowhere. As Greyam puffed on a cigarette, Bobby arched his back and dug his claws into Greyam's leg.

Just then, the ashtray on the shelf beside him flew across the room, shattering against the wall.

Greyam bolted up the stairs, emerging back into the warm pub, feeling a chill of fear he would never forget.

Later, when a customer remarked on his ashen appearance, Greyam could only manage a nervous laugh, but the experience left a lasting impression.

In November 1982, the BBC's 'Six O'clock Show' featured the Grenadier in a live segment about London's haunted pubs.

The pub staff were prepared to carry on as usual amidst the eerie green lighting and dramatic setup to enhance the haunted atmosphere.

Not long after, the in-house magazine for Grand Met (then the pub's parent company) shared stills from the evening.

One photograph captured everyone's attention: an indistinct but unmistakable face seemed to peer from one of the windowpanes.

Sceptical at first, they assumed it was a trick of light reflecting from an outdoor lantern or simply shadows from a nearby tree.

But when the photographer zoomed in, the face became clearer—a young man with a dark handlebar moustache, his head slightly turned as though looking directly at the camera.

Only one of the photos taken that night contained the haunting image, adding to the pub's mysteries.

For those who venture into the Grenadier today, it offers more than just a pint—it's an experience steeped in history, ghostly legends, and a spirit all its own.

Whether drawn by the supernatural or the historic charm, visitors to the Grenadier find themselves transported to another time, immersed in the tales of soldiers, gamblers, and spectral figures still haunting its walls.

As we close our tour of the Top Ten Haunted Pubs of the UK, we leave behind the dark histories, ghostly figures, and eerie legends that shape each of these remarkable inns and taverns.

From spectral apparitions lingering in centuries-old beams to haunted cellars echoing with whispers from the past, each pub tells a unique story, woven from tragedy, mystery, and a touch of folklore.

For centuries, these pubs have been more than just places to share a drink; they are living histories, where the line between the past and present blurs and the walls seem to hold memories of both joy and sorrow.

Whether you're a skeptic or a believer, visiting these haunted pubs is like stepping into another world—a world where time stands still, and the supernatural feels just a little more real.

So, should you ever find yourself in the cozy warmth of a centuries-old inn, take a moment to listen closely to the silence, let the shadows whisper their secrets, and toast to those who came before.

For in Britain's haunted pubs, history isn't just remembered; it lingers, as alive as the spirits that still haunt them.

Cheers to the spirits, seen and unseen, that make these pubs legends in their own right.